Hiawatha: Or The Story Of The Iroquois Sage, In Prose And Verse

Benjamin Franklin DeCosta

In the interest of creating a more extensive selection of rare historical book reprints, we have chosen to reproduce this title even though it may possibly have occasional imperfections such as missing and blurred pages, missing text, poor pictures, markings, dark backgrounds and other reproduction issues beyond our control. Because this work is culturally important, we have made it available as a part of our commitment to protecting, preserving and promoting the world's literature. Thank you for your understanding.

HIAWATHA:

OR,

THE STORY OF THE IROQUOIS SAGE

IN PROSE AND VERSE.

By Benjamin Franklin DeCosta

NEW YORK:
ANSON D. F. RANDOLPH & CO.
1873.

PREFACE.

In presenting the following observations and verses, the author does not desire to appear in the *rôle* of either critic or poet; the object being rather to indicate the belief that a new "Hiawatha" is among the possibilities of the future, a conviction which is offered in connection with a rhymed version of the Story of Hiawatha, as given in prose by a descendant of the Red Men skilled in the traditions of his race. The observations are presented in the way of helpful suggestions; while the verses, for which no merit is claimed, may at least add some interest to this *brochure*.

NEW YORK, 1872.

INTRODUCTORY.

THE Red Man in North America has alternately been the victim of the poet and politician. The wrongs suffered through the emissaries of the State may be of a more vital character than those inflicted by the Muse, yet they cannot be more real; for it has been the custom of the poet to clothe the Red Man in a histrionic garb, and invest him with exaggerated action. In literature he has, therefore, on the whole, had more than his due. The "Noble" overshadows the "Poor Indian." Still there have been exceptions to the general rule, and thus a great character has occasionally been allowed to stand far below the true level. This, perhaps, has been the case with Hiawatha, the Sage of the Iroquois.

In saying this, however, I have no desire to reflect upon the course adopted by Mr. Longfellow, in his beautiful poem of "Hiawatha." His representations are, in the main, based on Indian traditions. He has drawn the character of Hiawatha as the Red Men themselves have often represented it. Besides, he had a perfect right to choose his own point of observation. The liberty that the circumstances of the case afford has not been abused. He has simply selected those aspects best adapted for *pictorial* effect. Yet while this is an age in which we are accustomed to view a story on its most winning side, we are nevertheless entitled to the right of independent judgment, and the use of the same liberty accorded to the Poet, in an effort to present what appears to be a more probable view of the history of the great Iroquois Chief.

At a time like the present, it may appear a somewhat unpromising task to present Hiawatha as anything like a historic person, or seek to preserve the name from the atmosphere of grotesque fable. Yet this, perhaps, is a task that might be undertaken; for when we remember how easily, with the lapse of time, an individual, even in civilized society, becomes invested with an air of romance, we shall hardly feel inclined to question the existence of the tendency among rude and uncivilized tribes.

It has already been remarked that Mr. Longfellow was perfectly justified in presenting that view of the Indian Sage which he has given in his poem; still it will perhaps prove interesting to employ our liberty in making a brief comparison of the Indian who appears on his page with the Indian found among the better class of Algic traditions; that is, a comparison of Hiawatha as his character is popularly conceived, and Hiawatha as he possibly was.

INTRODUCTORY.

How, then, does the character of Hiawatha appear in the poem of Mr. Longfellow?

First, however, let us hear what Mr. Schoolcroft says of the sources of the poet's information.

In speaking of the legends upon which Mr. Longfellow has relied, the historian says, in substance, that they represent Hiawatha on the whole, as an impersonation of evil. The evil is not, indeed, without mitigation, yet the essential badness of Hiawatha is combined with low cunning, ineffable weakness, and the paltriest ambition. Consequently we find that the character which the poet represents, continually reminds us of its origin. Certain qualities may be depressed, and some may be exaggerated, while others may be left out altogether, and yet the feeble trickster is always there, holding himself up to view amid all the affluence of rhythm and imagery and art, as a compound of opposite and often contemptible qualities. This, once more let it be remembered, I state, not as a fault, but as a *fact*.

I might, perhaps, have been told at the outset that similar characters abound everywhere in history. There, for instance, is Josheka of the Algonquins; who finds a parallel, in turn, among the mythical creations of the distant South. Why not, then, place the story of Hiawatha with his? To this it may be replied that, while found among them, it is not of them. The story of Hiawatha evidently belongs to a more modern age, and is not by any means to be *properly* included in the class of myths at all. The story is essentially of the nature of a *legend*. It does not deal with a *quality*. It sets forth no trancendental truth. It rather tells the story of a life, and gives, seemingly, amid all its wild exaggerations, a modicum of historic truth. Let us, therefore, endeavor to make this more apparent.

In dealing with the native tribes of America, the historian has generally given almost exclusive prominence to the two branches that so strongly established themselves in Mexico and Peru. And yet the famous Confederacy of the Iroquois or Five Nations, was established not more than one or two centuries after the Mexican and Peruvian monarchies, and is quite as worthy, in many respects, of high consideration. Especially does this appear to be the case in connection with the present subject, for the reason that this Confederacy of the Iroquois was established by the agency of Hiawatha, a fact that Mr. Longfellow's poem does not bring to view. This brings the hero within comparatively modern times, somewhere near the thirteenth century.

Until about this period the five nations composing the league were widely scattered over large portions of the country. But an invasion from the north led them, under the guidance of Hiawatha, to unite for the extirpation of the common foe. The

League of the Iroquois was fashioned after the Greek Amphictyonic League, and while the union was real and practical, each of the five banded tribes was left with its separate and sovereign right. And so conscious were the Indian leaders of the wisdom and advantages of their system, that in the year 1774, they gravely urged it upon the representatives of the Colonies for the acceptance of the American people. Republicanism did not begin with Greece, nor was it the exclusive issue of the American Revolution. The white man may be slow to recognize the fact, yet it is nevertheless not too much to affirm, that essential republicanism in this country began with the League of the Five Nations, who were taught the advantages of the system by Hiawatha; all of which is worthy of finding expression in a peculiarly American poem.

What we may call the historic character of Hiawatha forms a distinct point which the writer desires to present and keep in view; and yet there is the separate inquiry, namely, whether we have ground for claiming a loftier character for Hiawatha, and one everyway more dignified and pure, than the conception now before the people.

The eccentric Thoreau used sometimes to wonder what it was in the character of Christ that made a certain bishop so bigoted. But Thoreau was not sure of his *fact*. There was not *anything* in the great heart of the Galilean to make a man bigoted. We may nevertheless inquire what there was in the character of Hiawatha to secure the Red Man's universal veneration. They certainly paid no respect to a *quality* under the form of a person, and therefore are we at liberty to infer that it was the *person himself*, in whom certain great qualities were found.

The version of the Indian legends which Mr. Longfellow has followed come from every quarter of North America, and are marked by all that is puerile, extravagant and ridiculous ; yet we have another version which is the peculiar product of the Iroquois mind, and therefore characterized by the same degree of superiority that must be confessed as attending the thoughts of the people of that Confederacy. This version of the story of Hiawatha is free from all that is low, puerile, sensual and absurd, and commands respect by its dignity, consistency and general effect. The style of the narrative is comprehensive, the contents brief, and thus the story is soon told.

From a consideration of the facts of the case, it would seem, therefore, as if there were room for a new Hiawatha. Yet when Hiawatha comes he must not be *too* historical. He must speak to us a long way off. His voice must come sounding down from the distant times. Here, then, might be suggested a substantial improvement on Longfellow's Hiawatha, where we have the

INTRODUCTORY.

Jesuits introduced without authority, and where they appear as appropriate as a band of Pilgrim Fathers would in one of the Books of Virgil. As Longfellow's Hiawatha is about to ascend to heaven, we read:

> "From the distant Land of Wabun,
> From the farthest realm of morning,
> Came the Black-Robe chief the Prophet,
> He the Priest of Prayer, the Pale face,
> With his guides and his companions.
>
> "And the noble Hiawatha,
> With his hands aloft extended,
> Held aloft in sign of welcome,
> Waited, full of exultation,
> Till the birch canoe with paddles
> Grated on the shining pebbles,
> Stranded on the sandy margin,
> Till the Black-Robe chief, the Pale face
> With the cross upon his bosom,
> Landed on the sandy margin."

This certainly is an anachronism, the flavor being too modern.

The statement of Mr. Schoolcraft has been cited where he claims that the legend followed by Mr. Longfellow represents Hiawatha largely as an embodiment of evil. And the Iroquois chief does not escape this taint altogether in passing through the alembic of the Poet. At the same time his positive religious character is everyway overstated. Hiawatha "fasting" in Longfellow's pages is one thing, and Hiawatha fasting in the legend is quite another. In the one case he is rigidly devout, and in the other he is overflowing with characteristic mischief and fun, stealing jovially away from his secluded praying lodge, to watch his grandmother, who surreptitiously, in his absence from home, entertains a huge black bear. But the legend quoted in the verses that follow do not treat of that matter at all.

In the Iroquois legends used in the present case, we look in vain for anything that essentially detracts from his dignity, goodness and worth; and, at the same time, the legend is free from anachronisms. Hiawatha does not enter into the thoughts of the seventeenth century, when the Jesuit roamed the American woods, and bought at any price the privilege of sending an Indian child to heaven with a drop of dew. The date of Hiawatha's death is synchronous with the perfect establishment of the Iroquois League, which had already arrived at the height of its glory, and was the dominant Indian power on the North American continent before the white man encroached upon the soil. The Iroquois tradition, indeed, confounds Hiawatha with the more uncertain Tarenyawago, yet he soon emerges in the narrative with a new name, and appears before the antiquary, as

INTRODUCTORY.

he probably was, bearing a lofty, consistent character, shedding equal lustre upon himself and upon the fortunes of his tribe. Such a character hardly deserves to be buried under the *débris* of ridiculous fable, or stand in the rank with Yennadizze the Idle. The Indian annals show only *one* such comprehensive and beneficent character, and, therefore, why not let the Red Man enjoy its benefit?

It may indeed be said that the character of Hiawatha, even as given by the Iroquois, is unreal; yet it should be remembered that a thirteenth-century myth could not well found a *government*, or administer laws. There must have been somewhere a powerful organizing mind—a real personality; for the work done was both permanent and great. All this implies a *great worker*. And may not that worker have been Hiawatha?

The conception of Hiawatha embodied in the following lines, is therefore offered as more consistent and dignified than that popularly entertained, and which makes the heaven-born Hiawatha appear contemptible, by reducing him, without reason, to all the ordinary straits of the Red Man, and leads him to desire conflicts he cannot support and dangers before which he quails. In the Iroquois version, the character of Hiawatha and the incidents of his life are always invested with unity and dignity. He never appears childish, but always bears himself with the aspect and temper of the sage. Indeed, the character is drawn so true to nature, that we are led to the conclusion that such a person of Hiawatha once lived, and that his course as a public teacher and benefactor in the after times led the Five Nations to invest him with supernatural wisdom and power, and to assign him a fitting end. Thus it was with the Northman's Odin, who, after dying in his bed, like an ordinary mortal, was nevertheless, in course of time, invested with the character and attributes of a god. And it is probable that Hiawatha was no more a myth than Odin, but that both were historical characters; Indian tradition having left the latter elevated high above the common walks of life, as given, beyond the ordinary race of mortals, to wise, heroic and beneficent deeds. Those persons inclined to doubt this, should endeavor to tell us who it was that formed the American Amphictyonic League; who gave the Iroquois legislation and laws; who, by the power of his genius, banded the Five Nations into one; and who, by the force of his example and the purity of his precepts, cemented the great fabric which stood for many generations in the heart of America as a refuge for those people not exactly included within the League, but who, nevertheless, as history declares, found it as refreshing in their day as the shadow of a great rock in a weary land.

HIAWATHA.

HIAWATHA.

TARENYAWAGO, from the West Wind sprung,
Revered in Council and in story sung,
A chief to Manitou allied by birth,
With his approval once appeared on earth,
To guide the Red Man by his counsels wise,
And ope the passage to immortal skies:
Hear, then, the story of the Wind-born[1] Sage,
The wondrous prophet of a distant age,
As told in wigwams on Tioga's shore
By ancient chieftains of the Iroquois.

THE BENEFACTOR.

Tarenyawago, through that North-land wide,
Whose woods and waters were the Red Man's pride,
Taught useful knowledge, and each cunning cure
That simples furnish or deep spells assure;
Showed how to foster the green-springing corn,
And beans bright-blossomed that the fields adorn,

Where gourds grew portly all the summer day,
And juicy melons in the sunshine lay.
The bubbling fountains he revealed with skill,
Deep dredged each streamlet, and explored each rill,
Made roomy passage for the finny tribe,
Then easy luréd by the fisher's bribe;
Slew furious monsters that o'er ran the land,
And thus gave safety to each roving band.
In wisdom, equal to his wondrous strength,
The race revered him through the land's great length,
And chiefs, who listened to his wholesome speech,
Oft foremost stations in the tribes would reach.
Tarenyawago also kindly gave
Alike to chieftain and to common brave,
Much deep instruction in the simple law
Revealed by Manitou for Iroquois.

THE MAGIC CANOE.

Where'er he journeyed, his light bark canoe,
In swift obedience without paddle flew;
His wish propelled it up the tugging stream,
And drove it onward where the rapids gleam,
To breast the eddies 'neath the granite wall,

To skim the surges, or to leap the fall.
On land, the birch-boat was obedient still,
And felt the magic of his wondrous will;
For at his bidding it quick rose to bear
Its mystic master on the trembling air,
And thus he darted through the sunny sky,
Where dizzy mountains in the haze rush by,
And over valleys clad in robes of green,
Which rivers broider with their silver sheen.

RETIREMENT.

Tarenyawago, when his work was done,
The people being to his teachings won,
Next laid the office of a seer aside,
Though sounding plaudits fill the North-land wide,
And seeks in private his short day to spend,
Until, predestined, his career should end:
For, with the precept, it is his to give
A life that teaches how the just should live.

HIAWATHA AT HOME.

His home, well-ordered, on Tioga's bank,
In style adapted to the humble rank,

Which Hiawatha 'mong the people bears,
The usual aspect of the Red Man wears.
Naught ever marks him from his neighbors round,
Except his sanctity and well-tilled ground,
Where all the husbandry that masters know
His faultless corn-fields in their culture show.
Yet ne'er he's wanting in the homage due,
For chiefs divided towards Tioga drew,
And came from regions both remote and near
To pour their cases in his patient ear.
Tarenyawago, him they cease to call,
But "Hiawatha," or, Surpassing All
In Lofty Wisdom, is the peerless name
They give to signify his rightful fame.

THE WOOING.

Touched by the passion e'en immortals share,
His heart was raptured by a maiden fair,
And soon, thus living, knew 'twould not be life
Without this maiden for his prudent wife.
By chaste advances, he makes known his love.
When Kibblaneno, or the Gentle Dove.
Dissimulation and concealment tries

With face averted and with down-cast eyes;
But tell-tale blushes soon perform their part,
When glad she nestles on her lover's heart.

THE WEDDING.

With tender watchfulness they bear his bride
Where stands the wigwam by Tioga's[2] side,
Adorned and furnished in becoming state
For Hiawatha and his gentle mate.
Three days of revels are next quickly spent,
With mirthful dances and high feasting blent;
Which done, the people take their homeward way,
And leave the lovers with the livelong day.

IN THE WIGWAM.

Then moons, oft waning, lost their silver sheen,
But in the wigwam, uneclipsed, was seen
The tender lustre of love's constant star,
Which flitting soul-clouds had no power to mar.
The Onondagas now ere long rejoice
To learn the wigwam knows a little voice.
Oft Hiawatha takes the welcome guest
And clasps her fondly to his manly breast;

And, while her soft eyes view life's early dawn,
Laloona names her, or the Little Fawn.
Thus years of plenty roll serenely by,
And tribes in hunting with each other vie;
While sweet Laloona, to a woman grown,
For gentle beauty and high worth is known.
Then from the water Hiawatha drew
His talismanic and far-famed canoe,
Nor used it ever, save when strong desire
Led the great Prophet to the council-fire.

THE WAR-PATH.

At last the limits of long peace drew near,
And all the borders were deep stirred by fear;
For hostile warriors from the Great Cold Lake
The southern war-path in fell fury take
In countless numbers, and the war-whoop rose
With vengeful fury from their ancient foes.
While 'mong the people spread the deep dismay,
The leaders, anxious, took their silent way
To Hiawatha, whom, serene, they found
Among the corn-rows of his well-tilled ground.
The issue stated, and his counsel sought:

The wise man warned them not to spend for naught
The people's courage, but united stand,
And meet the inroads of th' invading band;
Hence call a council, and a compact make
By Onondaga's deep, wide-spreading lake.

THE ASSEMBLY.

Thus Hiawatha his wise counsel gave,
Which, through the forest, flew from brave to brave.
Then quick each leader tribal aims forgot,
And marched with ardor to the chosen spot,
Where soon assembled a dark, bronzéd crowd
Of squaws and children and of chieftains proud,
Thus by misfortune to the council brought,
Each mind with projects of relief deep fraught.
But Hiawatha to the place ne'er came,
And expectation soon began to wane,
When envoys, going to Tioga's wood,
Where stayed the master in abstracted mood,
Told the great Prophet their unfeigned desire
To greet his presence at the council-fire.

THE JOURNEY.

Aroused, he enters his light bark canoe,
Which erst on water as on air swift flew,

His loved Laloona at the graceful prow,—
For ne'er he travels from Tioga now
Without the maiden, his great people's pride,
In whom brave chieftains vainly sought a bride.
First, slowly moving, with the stream they drift,
Till near the entrance of So-ha-ri's³ rift,
When Hiawatha, by the mystic spell,
Whose cunning magic it obeys full well,
His bark drove onward past the waving brake,
And swiftly enters Onondaga's Lake.
When seen approaching the long-circling shore,
By murky camp smoke high dull-bannered o'er,
The people wildly run the banks about
And raise their voices in a joyous shout.
The magic vessel now shoots up the strand,
While stalwart chieftains grasp the Prophet's hand,
And with such honor as the brave deems due
Receive Laloona from the light canoe.

THE BIRD OF FATE.

The Sage in silence toward the Council-place,
Then walks with dignity and high born grace,
Laloona moving with a regal mien,

That tells the presence of the Indian Queen.
But, scarce arriving on the moss-grown bank,
Where sits the Council in well-ordered rank,
A dreadful portent soon on high appears,
While muttered thunder smites on savage ears;
For, looking upward in the clear blue sky,
A white-plumed Eagle they now clear descry,
Which, first, a hand-breadth, next appears a cloud,
A bird, whose pinions e'en the sunbeams shroud,
A thing of monstrous and unseemly birth,
Now swooping swiftly toward the verdant earth.
Then soon pale terror strikes the tawny host,
Whose oft-tried courage was the people's boast,
For ranks of sachems now unseemly break,
And, flying, refuge in the deep woods take.

THE DEATH OF LALOONA.

But Hiawatha, calm, alone stood still,
Proud on the summit of the Council-hill,[4]
His peerless daughter by his aged side,
Prepared the issue of the hour to bide.
Yet Fate, who never to the wisest gave
The briefest respite, or the great and brave

Indulged one instant past the hapless hour,
Stays not for Beauty his relentless power;
For, as the comet trails the azure sky,
On rushing pinion the great bird draws nigh,
And, after circling through the mid-air round,
Smites fair Laloona to the mossy ground!
His beak transfixing her devoted breast,
Swift sends her spirit to the realm of rest.
But, see! the Eagle, is itself laid low,
Slain by the fury of the vengeful blow;
And thus, deprivéd of his lusty breath,
With powerless pinions he lies stretched in death.
The aged Prophet felt the air's dread rush,
And saw the life-blood from his daughter gush,
Yet, calm, he stirred not from his standing place,
Nor moved a muscle of his bronzéd face,
But saw serenely, as becomes the brave,
The awful judgment the Great Spirit gave.

THE VOW.

At distance, peering from a moss-grown rock,
Some frightened warriors felt the fatal shock,
And now, returning, they upheave the bird;

But marvels cease not, and they speak no word,
When 'neath the Eagle's white far-spreading wing,
Which six strong warriors now could scarce upfling;
No trace they noted of the lovely maid
Thus strangely summoned to the land of shade.
Then came each savage and with dreadful vow
Pluck'd a white feather for his painted brow,
And ever after on the war-path wore
This dread insignia of the Iroquois.[5]

IN COUNCIL.

When all was over and the sad truth known,
Great Hiawatha sat aside alone,
His soul keen smarting with the cutting grief,
For which the Prophet could find no relief.
But, called from sorrow by the people's woes,
Soon to the Council the great Sachem goes,
And, clad in wolf-skin, takes the master's seat,
Prepared the issue of the tribes to meet;
Hearing each caution that the wise men gave
With hot invective of the heady brave.
One day is given to discursive speech;
But when the issue on the next they reach,

Great Hiawatha, from his lofty place,
Slow rising, counsels with superior grace.

HIAWATHA'S SPEECH.

Friends, Brothers, Leaders of the valiant bands,
Whose wigwams cover our wide-spreading lands,
In vain you, singly, fight the dreaded foe,
Whose coming portends a great people's woe;
In vain you struggle with the Northern hordes,
While still you follow your divided lords:
Unite your forces for the common weal,
And thus your vengeance shall the foeman feel.
You, warlike Mohawks, 'neath the Tall Pine Tree,[6]
The first great power in the League shall be.
You, Brave Oneidas, 'gainst the Lasting Stone,
Recline the second, and ne'er fight alone.
You, Onondagas, by the Shelt'ring Hills,
With crags deep-fretted by the plunging rills,
Whose voice well-freighted with wise speech is heard,
Shall take your order in the League, the third.
Next, Senecas, who in the Wild-wood dwell,
And know each danger of the chase full well,
Superior Hunters, for your noble worth

In our great compact you shall stand the fourth.
And Wise Cayugas of the Open Field,
Whose grounds to culture give uncommon yield,
Well Housed, among us, you the fifth shall stand
In serried order with the common band:
To feebler people,[7] who for aid may call,
We give the friendship and the strength of all.
And thus, united, we shall honored be,
While all the borders of the land are free.
Rise, Braves! and arm you in united might,
And meet the foeman in the deadly fight,
Thus the Great Spirit on your League will smile,
And give you wisdom to meet every wile;
But scorn this counsel, and his awful frown
Shall blight each village and the sorrow crown,
While you, forgotten by our ancient race,
Shall fall unpitied from your honored place,
Enslaved and ruined by the ruthless foe,
Who now stands ready for the fatal blow.

THE CONFIRMATION.

Thus, Hiawatha: and each burning word
With deathless ardor the great Council stirred;

And, 'mid the tumult of prolonged applause,
The tribes pledged union for the common cause:
In days that followed the invader knew
What signal power from that compact grew.

THE TRANSLATION.

His mission ended to the sun-bright earth,
The Seer reminds them of his wondrous birth,
And, though the people his great presence prize,
Prepares to journey towards the distant skies.
Again he bids them with united voice,
Maintain the compact of their willing choice.
Much weighty counsel with his blessing gave,
With special caution to each heady brave;
Then, viewing sadly the Assembly o'er,
Walked down in silence to the sandy shore,
Assumed meet posture in the famed canoe,
Which still the magic of the Master knew,
Laid on the gunwale his thin, shrunken hand,
And slowly parted from the crowded strand.
First, moving lightly o'er the shining mere,
Borne by the power of the mighty Seer,
The bark went onward for a little way,

And passed the entrance of the golden bay;
Then rose majestic on the evening air,—
Slow sailing upward to those regions fair
That ope their portals to the setting sun,
With regal splendor when his course is run,—
While sweetest music filled each savage ear,
And swelled in peans such as angels hear.
Thus, Hiawatha neared the happy coast,
Of bright Owayne and his winged host;
When forth to meet him went a shining band
That led the Prophet to the Blessed Land.

Such is the story that a simple race
Oft told in wigwams with untutored grace;
Hence came the compact and far-reaching law
That bound the peoples of the Iroquois,
And when long ages had their cycle run,
The Great Five Nations left allied as One.

NOTES.

1, Page 16. Hiawatha's mother, a descendant of the daughter of the Moon, was susceptible to the influence of the West Wind, which became the father of Hiawatha, or "Manabozho."

2, Page 20. Tioga Lake is now called "Cross Lake." The Indian name was *Te-ungk-too*. It is reached by the Seneca River.

3, Page 23. So-ha-ri's rift is the passage through which the waters of the Onondaga Lake flow into the Seneca River, on its way to Lake Ontario.

4, Page 24. It is the unanimous opinion that the League of the Iroquois was formed on the bank of the Onondaga.

5, Page 26. The Eagle's feather is the sign of these banded tribes.

6, Page 27. The characteristics of each of the five tribes are given in accordance with the best authorities.

7, Page 28. A few lesser tribes that came under the patronage of the League are sometimes known as a *Sixth Nation*. A remnant of the Onondagas still remain in New York State, near Syracuse.

Printed by Libri Plureos GmbH in Hamburg, Germany